Streamline G

Le

Milo

Jennifer Bassett

Series Editors:
Bernard Hartley and Peter Viney

OXFORD UNIVERSITY PRESS

Oxford University Press
Walton Street, Oxford OX2 6DP

Oxford   New York
Athens   Auckland   Bangkok   Bombay
Calcutta   Cape Town   Dar es Salaam   Delhi
Florence   Hong Kong   Istanbul   Karachi
Kuala Lumpur   Madras   Madrid   Melbourne
Mexico City   Nairobi   Paris   Singapore
Taipei   Tokyo   Toronto

and associated companies in
Berlin   Ibadan

OXFORD and OXFORD ENGLISH are
trade marks of Oxford University Press

ISBN 0 19 421926 7

Illustrated by: Alan Marks
Cover illustration by: Sophie Williams

Typeset by Pentacor Ltd, High Wycombe, Bucks
Printed in Hong Kong

My dear Lola,

I feel a little strange, writing this letter to you, as you will not read it until I have been dead for many years. I am now an old woman of seventy-seven years, but you are only ten, and still a child. In fact, as I write this, I can see you outside in the garden, playing in the snow with my brother Michael's grandchildren. You have built a snowman under the apple tree, but it is not a very good one and I think it will collapse quite soon. There is a lot of laughing and shouting, and running around . . . and some very wet clothes! I don't know a better way for children to spend a bright winter's day.

So do not be sad, my dear granddaughter, when you read this. You are my only grandchild, and your life will continue long after mine has finished. Because of this, I want you to read the story in this notebook. I wrote it long before you were born, and it is about something that happened fifty-two years ago, in the summer of 1998. A hot summer, I remember . . . and a very strange one.

I know that I don't have long to live – my heart is not strong – but you are much too young now to listen to such a story. So I have told my lawyers to give you this notebook and my letter when you are twenty-five.

It's not a long story, Lola, so be patient with me, and read it carefully. Every word of it is true.

12th November 1998

My name is Sally Gardiner. I am a school teacher, and I live and work in the small town of Moreton in Devonshire – a quiet, sleepy town on the edge of Dartmoor. Nothing much happens in Moreton; the people are friendly but they are suspicious of change and of the outside world. Unless you are born here, you are a 'foreigner' until the day you die.

Both my parents and grandparents were born in or near Moreton, and all my family live here – I have four younger brothers, and more cousins than I can remember – and I enjoy being part of a large and noisy family.

However, it is sometimes *too* noisy, even for me, so I live on my own, in a small cottage just outside the town. But there are always people coming and going from my parents' house or my uncle's farm. No one can be lonely in a family like mine.

That was how things were last summer – the summer of 1998. I was twenty-five, enjoyed my teaching job, had plenty of friends, and nothing at all to worry about.

It was in June that I first met Milo. It was hot, dry weather. My youngest brother, Tom, was staying with me at the time. He was fourteen, and was supposed to be studying for an exam. But Tom spent more time out on his bicycle or fishing with friends than he did working on his books.

That Saturday I woke up very early. I had turned over to go back to sleep again when I heard voices outside my window. It was my brother Tom and Old Bill Hayes, my neighbour.

'Morning, young Tom. Going fishing, are you?' Old Bill was a retired farmworker and lived in the cottage next to mine. He was about seventy-eight years old, but his voice was still loud and clear.

I heard my brother whispering something, but I could not hear the words.

Old Bill laughed. 'Go on!' he said. 'I don't believe you, boy. Your sister wouldn't make you work on your books on a lovely morning like this.'

I could not hear my brother's reply, but I suspected it was not very polite.

Old Bill laughed again. 'You'd better hurry then. I'll tell Sally you took your books with you.'

I heard Tom's bicycle going down the road, and then I got out of bed and went to the window.

'You shouldn't encourage him not to work, Bill,' I called down to him. 'He'll never pass his exam.'

Old Bill looked up at my window. 'Ah, come on,' he said. 'You're only young once. Let the boy enjoy himself. It's Saturday, isn't it? And look at the weather. You don't get many days like this.'

I looked out and up at the sky. It was a bright, clear blue. It was going to be a hot, still day. Old Bill was right. It was too good to stay inside. I dressed quickly, and ran out of the cottage, up onto the path that led to the open moor.

People say that Dartmoor is the last wild place in England.

You can walk for hours and never see a house or a village. In winter it is a hard, cruel place, when the cold east winds whistle and scream across the empty hills, and the snow falls two metres deep and more. But in summer the moor can be a place of great beauty, with its bright flowers and the clear brown water of its rivers and streams.

I was going to one of those streams now. I had discovered it long ago. The stream ran over some steep rocks and fell down into a small pool below. Round the pool, in a tiny valley, grew a few small trees and many bright green water plants. The valley was completely hidden. It was a secret, magic place. I had never seen anyone else there.

I got there after an hour's walk, and went and sat beside the pool and put my hands down into the cool water. The sun was still low in the sky, and there were long shadows across the water of the pool. The only sound was of water falling over the rocks.

And then I saw the boy. He was sitting on the other side of the pool in the shadow of a tree. He sat quite still, watching me.

I sat up suddenly. 'Goodness,' I said. 'You gave me a fright. I didn't see you there.'

'I'm sorry,' the boy said slowly. 'I didn't want to frighten you.'

'That's all right,' I said cheerfully. 'You're the first person I've ever seen here. How did you find the place?'

'I just . . . found it,' he said. 'I wasn't looking for it.'

'Well, we'll have to share the secret now,' I said, and smiled at him. 'But you mustn't tell anyone else about it.'

'Oh no,' he said, very seriously. 'I won't do that.' He got up and came and sat on the edge of the pool.

I looked at him with interest. He was about ten or eleven years old, with straight fair hair and very blue eyes. His clothes looked like some kind of school uniform, but I did not recognize it.

'I don't think I know you,' I said. 'I know most of the children round here because I teach at Moreton School. Are you on holiday in Devonshire?'

He looked at me, and then suddenly he smiled for the first time.

'You don't look like a teacher,' he said. 'You look too young.'

I laughed. I have red curly hair and am not very tall. My brother, Michael, who is twenty-one, always tells me that I look about sixteen.

'Actually,' I said, 'I'm twenty-five, and I've been a teacher for three years.'

The boy looked at me curiously. 'What do you teach?' he asked. His fair hair fell over his eyes and he brushed it back.

'French. English. A bit of maths.'

He looked interested. 'What kind of maths?'

I was surprised. Most boys of his age did not want to talk about school lessons. The latest video, yes. Or the football scores. But not maths. Anyway, I told him about the maths lessons I gave to the ten-year-olds at the school.

He stared at me. 'Is that all?' he asked.

I did not understand him. 'It's a lot to do in a year,' I said. 'Some of the children find it very difficult.'

The boy looked at me, and then down at the pool. He said nothing, and seemed sad and lost in thought. He was a very strange little boy, and when he spoke, he seemed much older than his years. I was beginning to be rather curious about him.

'Where do you go to school?' I asked.

He did not reply, and bent over to put his fingers in the pool. The sunlight fell on his fair hair and it shone like gold. The sun had climbed in the sky and it was beginning to get hot.

Perhaps he was shy. I tried again. If he wanted to talk about maths, then we would talk about maths. Perhaps he was one of those very clever children with brains like computers.

'What do you do in *your* maths lessons, then?' I asked.

He told me. He talked for several minutes and explained carefully and in detail the kind of maths that Einstein might have known about, but not many other people. I was astonished.

'And what else do you learn at your school?' I asked.

He told me. I became more and more astonished. He also told me how hard he worked. Ten hours of lessons a day, six days a week. It was not surprising that he sounded like an old man. I thought of my brother Tom, who complained if he had to do more than two hours' work a day.

I told the boy this, and he became very interested. So I told him all about my brothers. About Michael, who wanted to be a doctor. About Roger, who played in a pop group. About Colin, who wanted to be a farmer. And about Tom, who did not want to be anything at all if he had to work at it. The boy smiled at this. He asked a lot of questions about me and my family, but he would not answer any questions about himself.

Then suddenly he looked at his watch and stood up. 'I have to go,' he said. 'Lessons begin in half an hour.'

'So where is your school?' I asked in surprise.

'It's at Batworthy, on the moor,' he said slowly, watching my face.

'I've never heard of it.' I stood up, and smiled at him. 'You'd better hurry. You'll be late.'

'Yes.' He turned to go.

'I often come here in the early morning,' I said. 'I'll probably come tomorrow. Will I see you here?'

He turned and looked at me. His face was still and serious. 'I don't know.'

'This place is our secret,' I encouraged him. 'I won't tell anyone. And I'm Sally. What's your name?'

'Milo,' he said slowly. Then he turned and quickly climbed up the rocks out of the little valley. By the time I had climbed to the top, he had disappeared.

I woke up very early again on Sunday. It was another beautiful morning. Tom was still in bed. He had begged me not to tell our parents about his day's fishing.

'They'll hear about it from somebody else,' I had said. 'You can't keep secrets in a small town like this.'

On my way up to the moor, I wondered if Milo would be there. Milo . . . a strange name for a strange boy. I wanted to find out more about him.

And he *was* there. He watched me as I climbed down the rocks into the valley.

'Hello,' he said, and gave me a slow, shy smile. He looked quite pleased to see me. I wondered if he was lonely at his school. I thought I would invite him back to the cottage to meet Tom. He was a lot younger than Tom, but you never know with children. They might become friends, or they might hate each other as soon as they met.

I sat down on the rocks and took my shoes off. The water was cool on my hot feet.

'It's going to be hot again,' I said. 'Is Sunday your free day? Why don't you come home with me and meet my brother Tom?'

'Oh no,' he said quickly. 'I can't do that. I have to be back at school by nine o'clock.' He sounded afraid, almost frightened. I wondered why.

'Oh, well, never mind,' I said calmly. 'It was only an idea.'

There were a few fish at the bottom of the pool. We watched them together. Then I asked him about his family. 'Do you go home to your parents in the holidays? And where do they live?'

He looked down at his feet in the pool, and moved them slowly from side to side.

'I don't have any parents,' he said.

'Oh, Milo,' I said quickly. 'I *am* sorry. I didn't know . . .'

'No,' he replied, and smiled. 'How could you know? I don't have any brothers and sisters either. That's why I like hearing about your family. Tell me some more about them.'

I did not like to ask him what had happened. Were both his parents dead? Had he ever known them? He did not seem upset, but he was very interested in my family.

'Tell me some more about Roger,' he suggested. 'And Tom.'

We talked, sitting on the rocks by that peaceful hidden pool, with only the empty wild hills of the moor around us. I told Milo many stories about my family and my life in Moreton. He listened, and laughed, and almost began to seem like other boys of his age. But I still had the strange feeling that I was talking to a much older person. He wanted to hear more and more about me and my family, but again, whenever I asked him questions about himself, he avoided answering.

Soon he stood up to go. 'Will you be here next weekend?' he asked. His eyes searched my face, looking for something. I didn't know what. 'I can only get out at weekends,' he explained.

I wondered again what kind of school he was at. 'OK,' I said. 'Saturday morning. Seven o'clock. I'll be here.'

During that week I tried to find out more about Milo's school. Batworthy was a tiny place on the edge of the moor – only a few houses really. Nobody had heard of a school there. I telephoned various people in various offices, but I didn't learn anything until I asked the head teacher at my own school. Mrs Martin had been teaching in Moreton for thirty-five years, and she knew everything about the people there.

'It must be a very small private school, Sally,' she said. 'There's a big old house just outside Batworthy. The school must be there. Strange place to have a school. It's a very lonely house. I don't know who owns it, but I think John Worrall looks after the house for the owner.'

Mr Worrall was a lawyer in Moreton. He was not very popular in the town. My father did not like him. 'If you ever want some friendly advice,' he once told me, 'don't go to John Worrall.'

However, I did not want advice; I wanted information. So on Tuesday I went to see Mr Worrall. He was cold and unhelpful.

He told me that some people had rented the house. They were paying a lot of money for it because they wanted to be private. He did not know who they were, or what they were doing.

He would not tell me anything else. And no one else could tell me anything.

On Wednesday my brother Michael came round to see me. I told him about Milo's strange school, and how no one seemed to know anything about it.

'Why don't you go up there and have a look?' Michael asked.

'Well, I don't like to, really, without asking Milo first. He might think I was a . . .'

'. . . a busybody?' said Michael, grinning.

'Thank you, Michael,' I said. 'You say such nice things! I am *not* a busybody!'

Michael laughed and finished his coffee. 'Well,' he said, 'you've looked for official information and haven't found any. Why don't you try unofficial information? Ask Old Bill. He keeps his ear to the ground.'

It was a good idea, so I did exactly that. News often travels in mysterious ways among country people, and on Friday evening Old Bill came round to my cottage.

'I had a word with old Jean Nuttall,' he told me. 'She lives up on the moor. Strange woman. Goes out a lot on the moor at night. Don't know what she does. Anyway, she says it's a very small, special school for children with – what was it? – learning difficulties.' Old Bill touched his head with his finger. 'You know, not quite right in the head. She says the gates are always locked, and she's never seen anyone going in or out. And she says she's seen a helicopter landing there at night.' Old Bill laughed. 'Helicopters! The woman's a bit mad herself, if you ask me.'

I thought about all this as I went up on the moor the next morning. If Milo had 'learning difficulties', I certainly had not noticed them. I had never met a more intelligent boy. What exactly was this school, and who was Milo? It was all very strange.

I knew I had to be careful. I liked Milo, but I knew he would not trust me if I started to be – well, a busybody. And if you want children to tell you things, it is usually better not to ask too many questions. If you are patient, and just listen and wait, you usually find out what you want to know.

But Milo, I was beginning to realize, was not an ordinary

child. His brain was as sharp as a knife, and he did not want to tell me anything about himself or his school, or his friends (did he have any?) or his teachers. And when I suggested that I might come to the school, he became very frightened.

'You mustn't do that,' he said quickly. 'Please. You said this place was a secret. You said you wouldn't tell anyone. Promise me you won't come to the school or tell anyone.' The blue eyes were full of fear as he watched me.

'All right,' I said gently. 'I promise. I won't go to your school, and I won't tell anyone about our valley.'

My four younger brothers had taught me that it was very important to keep promises. After a few minutes he became calm again, and we talked of other things, until the sun climbed in the sky and he had to go.

And so June turned into July, and then into August. The weather continued unusually hot and dry, and up on the moor the earth was as hard as rock. The pool in our little valley became smaller and smaller; the water plants turned brown and died in the heat of the sun.

I met Milo in our secret valley nearly every Saturday and Sunday morning, very early, before most of the world was awake. It was the only time he could get out of the school, he explained, without being seen. I had stopped asking questions, and usually spent most of the time answering Milo's questions.

He was hungry for details about everyday life, about ordinary family life, about my life as a student – about everything, in fact. Sometimes I took old family photographs to show him; and newspapers, and magazines, and books – especially children's books. He was very interested in those. I suppose he never saw them at his strange school.

It was a strange friendship. Sometimes we were like mother and son, sometimes sister and brother. On some days Milo was cheerful and laughed a lot; on other days he was sad and thoughtful and spoke like an old man of eighty. I did not really understand him at all. But I knew one thing about him – he was lonely. I seemed to be his only friend.

One Sunday morning in August, I was drinking coffee in my kitchen before going up to the moor to meet Milo, when Tom and Michael appeared at my back door.

'We're going fishing,' Tom said, as they came in. 'But we need some more breakfast first.'

'Well, I've got some cake,' I said. 'You can have some of that, I suppose. What about you, Michael?'

'Coffee, please,' said Michael. 'Where are you going, Sal? Up to the moor to meet Milo?'

'Sally's got a secret boyfriend,' said Tom, his mouth full of cake. 'He's not a schoolboy at all. He's about forty years old. He's tall, dark, good-looking and . . .'

'Don't be silly, Tom,' I said. Michael laughed.

Tom took another piece of cake before I could stop him. 'I'm going to tell William,' he said. William was my boyfriend. He was an engineer and was working in Scotland that summer, so we did not see each other very often.

'I expect the man on the moor is very rich, too,' Tom continued. 'Lots of money. And he's . . .'

'Oh, be quiet!' I said loudly. 'And stop eating my cake. Go away! Go and fall in a river!'

Tom laughed and ran to the door, taking the rest of my cake with him. Michael followed him. 'Thanks for the coffee,' he called. 'I'll push Tom in the river, shall I?'

'Yes please!' I called back, and waved goodbye to them both.

When I got to the secret valley, Milo was not there. He arrived soon afterwards, but he was quiet and seemed worried. We talked for a few minutes, but Milo was not really listening. Suddenly he said:

'I think I must go back now, Sally. I think someone . . . someone might have seen me.'

'But it's Sunday,' I said. 'Can't you ever do what you like? Everybody's got to have some time to themselves.' Suddenly I was angry. 'Your school is a terrible place. It's like a prison!'

'Yes,' said Milo very quietly. 'Perhaps it is a prison.' He bent his head so that I could not see his face.

'Milo,' I said quickly, 'we must do something. Can't I . . .'

He stood up suddenly. 'No. I must go.' He turned and began to climb up the rocks. Then he looked back at me.

15

'Will you be here next Saturday, Sally?'

'Yes, of course,' I called after him. 'And you know where my cottage is. You can come there any time . . .'

But he had gone, climbing quickly up the rocks and over the top on to the moor.

I sat down to think. I stared at the dead plants by the pool, but did not see them. I saw instead a small figure running quickly and silently over the moor . . . like a hunted animal. What was chasing him? Or who?

I waited a couple of days before I went to the school, in case Milo had got into trouble on the Sunday. I thought of a plan. I would pretend not to know Milo, or anything about him. I would say that I was a teacher at Moreton School (which was true), and that my school wanted to invite the children at Batworthy School to some sports afternoons (which was not true, but I was sure Mrs Martin would agree to it). I planned very carefully what I would say.

But I wasted my time. I did not get into the school, or even speak to anybody.

The school was not easy to find. I drove up and down the narrow little roads, and finally found the house by chance. There was no sign or name on the tall iron gates, and there was a high stone wall all round the very large gardens.

The gates were locked, and I could see very little through them as most of the house was hidden behind trees and bushes.

I called through the gates, 'Hello? Is anybody there?' but nothing happened and nobody came. I walked round the walls, but I could not see another gate. I came back to the front gates and called again, more loudly. Silence. I shook the gate angrily. The place seemed more and more like a prison.

I suddenly began to feel that I was being watched. But by whom? I stared into the trees, but there was nobody there.

After about half an hour of calling, and waiting and watching, I went home to think of another plan.

I decided to telephone the Department of Education in London. Weren't there rules about what could or could not be done in private schools? But the man who answered the phone was no help. He said that anyone could open a private school, but that if the children were of school age, officials from the Department would go to look at the school every few years.

'And have they been to the school at Batworthy?' I asked. 'It's been open for almost a year, I think.'

The man on the other end of the phone sounded tired. 'There are thousands of private schools in this country,' he explained patiently. 'We can't visit them all every year. Is there a problem with this school at Patworthy?'

'BATworthy,' I said loudly. 'B for Bravo. I don't know if there's a problem or not. But I think there might be. I think . . .'

'If there *is* a problem,' he interrupted me, 'we shall find it when we visit.'

And that was all he would say. He just wasn't interested.

That Saturday I got to the valley even earlier. As I waited by the pool in the early morning half-light, I wondered if I was worrying about nothing. But Milo's school did seem a very mysterious place, and I did not like mysteries.

I heard a noise behind me, and turned to look.

'Milo!' I called cheerfully. 'Hi! How're things?'

He came and sat down beside me.

'I haven't much time, Sally,' he began in a hurry. 'I have to get back. But I had to come and tell you. I can't come again. This is the last time.'

'But why, Milo? What's the matter? What's happened?'

'You came to the school, Sally. I asked you not to. And the video cameras saw you at the gates. The teachers showed us the video film and watched our faces to see if any of us recognized you. I don't think my face showed anything, but I'm not sure. And they're watching me very carefully now. It'll be too dangerous for me to come out again.'

There was a lot here that I did not understand. 'But why . . .' I began.

'I'm not allowed to go outside the school,' Milo explained. 'None of us are. The gates are controlled by computer and watched by video cameras. But I learnt how to change the computer program so that there was no record when I went out or came in. It's quite easy to do, if you know how.'

'Yes,' I said weakly, 'yes, I expect it is. But *why* can't you go out? Why is your school so secret, so like a prison?'

'If I tell you, you won't believe me,' said Milo slowly. His blue eyes watched me sadly, and there was no hope in his young face. My heart suddenly ached for him.

'Try me,' I said, smiling. 'I can believe *two* impossible things before breakfast.'

A quick smile came and went on his face. He looked down at the pool for a minute, then turned to me, and began:

'I know you think I am different from the children you teach. And I am – more different than you can imagine. I am part of a . . . a scientific experiment. I have no parents because . . . because I was "made" by scientists. My "mother" was a glass bottle in a science laboratory. And the purpose of this experiment is to produce people who are much more intelligent than ordinary people. This is done by genetic engineering – by mixing the genes. For these babies made in a laboratory, the scientists choose only the right kind of genes – you know, the things that decide how clever you are, what colour your eyes are, whether you're tall or short. Normally, of course, people can't choose their genes; they get a mix of genes from their parents and . . .'

'Yes, Milo,' I said quietly, watching him. 'I know what genes are.'

He hurried on, not looking at me. 'Well, there are quite a lot of us. And we are being trained to make the best use of our special brains. That is why we study so hard. We have the best teachers in the world – famous people from all the sciences. We will become the leaders of tomorrow's world, the men and women of power.'

Milo stopped, and brushed the hair out of his eyes. But before I could say anything, he continued with his astonishing story.

'The experiment began about ten years ago. We are the first of the "laboratory" children, and we are taught to be proud of it. But we are told never, never, never to talk to ordinary people. They won't believe us, or if they do, they'll be afraid of us, and will try to stop the experiment. Well, I've broken that rule. I've told you. And you don't believe me.'

He stopped, and in the silence between us the noise of the stream sounded unnaturally loud.

'It *is*,' I said carefully, 'quite a lot to believe . . . especially on a Saturday morning.'

Milo turned to look at me. He was quite calm and sensible, and very serious. 'It's true, Sally. Doesn't it explain all the things you haven't understood?'

'I suppose it does,' I admitted. 'But I don't understand how, or where, or who . . .'

'There's an international group of scientists. They began the experiment, and they keep it very, very secret. They're afraid people won't like it. So they keep us – the "new world" children, they call us – in small groups and move us about from country to country. There are, or were, twenty in my group, and we've lived in seven different countries. We don't belong anywhere, and we're always kept in schools like prisons.'

'But don't the children try to escape?' I asked.

'No. Why should they? They know they're different, and special. They don't want to be with boring, ordinary, "natural" people. They know they have a life of success and power in front of them, and they want to get on with it.'

'They're not going to be very nice people, are they?'

'No, I don't suppose they are. But that's not important to them. Their purpose in life is to be successful, not to be loved.'

'But what about you, Milo? You're different. You're not like that.'

'Yes. I think they made a mistake in the mix of my genes. I ask the wrong kind of questions. I break rules. And I *want* to be ordinary. I don't want power. I'd like to live in a family like yours, and go fishing with Tom in the morning.'

Milo stared into the pool. He sounded sadder than I had ever heard him sound before.

'But why can't you? There's nothing wrong in that!'

'Oh, there is, Sally. If I refuse to behave like the others, I might become a danger to them. I might talk to people like you.' He gave me a quick smile. 'There was a girl in our group . . . Evalina,' he continued. 'She could draw the most wonderful pictures. She was very, very good at it, and clever at a lot of other things, too. But sometimes she went crazy. She used to shout and scream, and throw herself about. Nobody could stop her. And she got worse and worse. Then one day last year she disappeared. I think they killed her.'

I stared at Milo. I was beginning to wonder if this was a bad dream.

'But Milo, that's . . . that's murder! It's not . . . They can't do that!'

'Can't they? She was part of an experiment that went wrong. And who's going to stop them? Her parents?'

Milo's intelligent eyes looked at me calmly. I began to feel terribly afraid.

'Milo,' I said quickly, 'I'm . . . Listen. You must come home with me now. At once.'

'No, Sally,' Milo said, in his quiet little voice. 'I knew you would say that. But I can't. Please don't come to the school again, or try to see me. I don't belong to your world. I could never belong to it now. I shall always be . . . different. So I have to go back. But I'm going to be careful now – much more careful. They won't catch me. I'm just as clever as they are.'

'Oh, Milo,' I cried, 'I know you are. But you're only a boy. You can't fight the whole world on your own!'

His eyes were too bright. He was near to tears. I reached out my hand towards him, but suddenly he got to his feet, and before I could stop him, he was climbing quickly up the rocks out of our valley.

I jumped up. 'Milo! Wait!' I called urgently, but by the time I had got to the top, he was away – running like the wind across the empty moor. Running too fast for me to catch him.

At home I tried to think calmly about what had happened. I felt as if I had been hit on the head – I did not know what to think. One minute I was going to drive up to the school, and rescue Milo at once from these terrible people. The next minute I did not believe Milo's story at all; it was just impossible, unreal, mad. The thoughts went round and round in my head. Did I believe Milo, or didn't I? If I did, what was I going to do about it?

Use your head, I told myself. Think. What's the sensible thing to do? Get advice. Talk to someone. Who? Not family. Who then? Someone who knows about . . . Yes! Angela!

I reached for the telephone at once. I had been at school with Angela, and she was now a very successful scientist, working in a famous laboratory in London. She would be able to tell me if genetic engineering with people was possible. That would be a start.

But Angela was away at a wedding, I learnt. She would be back by lunch-time on Sunday. I decided to drive up to London and wait for her to get back. It would be easier than talking over the phone.

I wish now I had not done that. But it is easy to be wise after something has happened. At the time, I thought I was being sensible.

Angela was surprised to see me, but even more surprised at my questions. She told me that astonishing things could be done nowadays with genetic engineering. New kinds of plants were 'made' every year, and there had been some successful experiments with farm animals, but every country in the world had laws to prevent experiments with people. It was scientifically possible to 'make' people, but of course no one did it.

By the time I got home that Sunday it was already dark. It had been a long drive and I was very tired and worried. So I groaned when I saw Old Bill coming towards me as I opened my front door.

'Ah, there you are,' he called. 'I've got a bit of news for you.'

I tried to look interested and hoped it was not a long bit of news.

'That school up on the moor – at Batworthy,' Bill began.

Suddenly I was very much awake. 'What about it?' I said.

The old man nodded, pleased at my interest. 'They've gone,' he announced. 'Packed up and gone. Went last night. Jean Nuttall told me.'

I stared at him. 'But . . . But they can't have gone . . .'

'Well, they have.' Old Bill nodded again. 'Nobody left in the place. Disappeared. The whole lot of them.'

I turned round and got back in my car. I drove as fast as I could up to Batworthy. But Old Bill was right. The gates were open and there were no lights anywhere. In the moonlight I walked up through the trees and stood, staring up at the house. The windows, dead and empty, stared back at me. There was no one there. Not even a ghost.

I never saw or heard of Milo again.

1st January 2050

And why – perhaps you are asking, my dear Lola – does my story stop there? What happened next, I hear you ask.

The answer is nothing. Of course, I tried very hard to find out what happened to the school at Batworthy . . . and to Milo. I telephoned people, I wrote letters, I asked questions, but nobody could tell me anything . . . or they would not tell me anything. The police would not look for Milo. Officially, there was no such person. He had no name, no family; there was no record of his birth.

People told me I was crazy. Things like that – 'laboratory' children – just could not happen. Milo, they said, was either mad, or he told lies to make himself interesting. In the end, I came to believe that Milo was probably just a sad little boy who lived in a dream world of his own. So I wrote down the story you have just read, Lola, put it away, and got on with my life. In later years, if I remembered Milo at all, I thought how silly I had been to believe him.

But now, I am not so sure. I look around me, and wonder. I have had a very busy life, but after I retired from teaching and after William – your grandfather – died, I had more time to watch, and listen, and think. And I begin to see a new kind of people in the world, who are hard and clever, and successful at everything they do.

So much of our lives is controlled by computers now, but these are the people who control the computers. They design the computers and write the programs, and they control the information that goes into and comes out of the computers. They have more and more power over us – and they are very different from the ordinary, 'natural' people that Milo spoke of. They even look like each other; they are always tall and good-looking . . . and you never hear anything about their families. Who are they? Where do they come from?

I think Milo told me the truth, Lola. I think these are the 'new world' people, made in laboratories with carefully chosen genes, and trained to use their brains but never to listen to their hearts. 'Their purpose in life,' Milo said, 'is to be successful, not to be loved.'

It must have taken a long time to get it right. Perhaps in the early days they made too many mistakes – like Milo. But in fifteen years' time, when you read this, Lola, there will be more and more of these 'new world' people. I think it will be a dangerous and frightening world to live in. When you begin such things, where do you stop?

Take great care, Lola . . . great care.

Your loving grandmother

Lola closed her grandmother's old notebook and stood up. She walked over to the window, and stood there, looking out at the evening sky. An air taxi flew quietly past the window to an air station on a nearby roof.

What a strange story, she thought. Her grandmother had died when she was twelve, but she remembered her quite clearly. She was a strong, kind woman and she was always ready for a game. And her house in Devonshire had always been full of people, usually relatives of one kind or another. Lola had spent many happy holidays there. That Christmas holiday fifteen years ago, she remembered, the house had been full of cousins, all rushing in and out with snow on their boots.

But it was a long time ago. Her grandmother had seemed such a sensible woman. But she must have imagined all that about Milo and the school on the moor for 'new world' children. It was a ridiculous idea.

The tiny television screen on her wrist flashed twice. Sim's face appeared. 'I'm home,' his voice said. 'I'm coming up.' Lola smiled. Sim was her husband. She had met him only six months ago, and three months later they were married. She went over to the wall and pushed the button to open the door in the hall.

Later that evening Lola gave Sim her grandmother's notebook to read. She watched him while he read. He read very quickly, much faster than she did. But then he did everything better than she did. Lola was a computer engineer, and a very good one, but Sim designed computers and their programs. He was very clever, and usually five ideas in front of other people. Everyone said he would go to the top.

Sim put the notebook down, looked at Lola, and laughed.

'Well, well, well,' he said. 'Who would have thought your grandmother knew about it sixty-seven years ago?'

'Knew about it? But it's not true, is it? It can't be.'

'Of course it's true, darling! You're married to one! Didn't you know?' He laughed again.

Lola stared at him. 'You mean you're . . .' She did not know how to say it.

Sim came and sat beside her. 'Yes, darling. Like Milo, I was made in a laboratory, not born. But they're getting much better at it now, you know. I believe they made quite a lot of mistakes in the early days.'

'But . . .' began Lola. There were too many questions she wanted to ask. She chose an easy one. 'Why didn't you tell me?'

'I thought you knew,' said Sim, smiling. 'It's not such a big secret now as it was in your grandmother's day. And why do you think I've been so successful? I'm more than halfway to the top already, and I'll control half the computer systems in the country before I'm thirty.' He stopped for a moment. 'What are you upset about? You're coming with me to the top.'

Lola looked at her grandmother's notebook. The writing had faded after so many years and the paper was brown at the edges. 'It isn't . . . natural,' she said.

'Don't be silly,' laughed Sim. 'Of course your grandmother

was afraid of the idea. But that was a long time ago. We're modern people, living in 2065. There's nothing unnatural about it – just a little help from the scientists, that's all. Why fill the world with stupid people when you can make clever ones?'

Lola said nothing for a minute or two. The ideas chased each other round in her head.

'What happens,' she said slowly, 'when the world is full of these . . . clever people?'

'Well, of course, genetic engineering is only for the top people,' Sim said impatiently. 'We don't want a world full of clever people. That would be a great mistake. No, genetic engineering makes sure that the right kind of people have power. People whose brains didn't happen by chance. People who know what to do, and how to do it . . . and who can protect and control the lives of ordinary people.'

'But perhaps,' said Lola, 'ordinary people would rather control their own lives.'

'Don't be ridiculous, Lola. Life today is much too difficult. Mr and Mrs Ordinary just go from one mistake to the next. They live in a prison of their own mistakes. We want to make their lives better. Genetic engineering is the most sensible thing that's happened for years. And ordinary people, of course, can continue to have children in the usual way.'

Lola looked at him. 'I thought we were going to have children – a family.' There was a small, cold feeling inside her. She was sure she remembered them talking about it before they were married.

'Oh, I don't think we want to do that, do we?' Sim smiled. 'We'll be too busy, anyway. And I want power . . . not a lot of noisy children under my feet. And nor do you. You want to be successful in your work, don't you?'

It was true, Lola thought. Her work was very important to her. But . . . Perhaps Sim would think differently in a few years' time. Or would he? He had never had a family life. The cold feeling inside her grew. She remembered again her grandmother's house in Devonshire. She suddenly thought of her grandmother's brother, Michael. He had been an old man, of course, when she knew him, but his hair was still bright red. Her grandmother's hair had turned quite grey – they used to joke about it with each other. There had always been a warm feeling in that house, she remembered. A family feeling. Natural.

She realized that Sim was watching her. She got up and walked across to the window, then turned to look at him. 'But families are . . . are part of nature . . .' She stopped. She felt she was not choosing the right words.

Sim picked up her grandmother's notebook, looked at it, and threw it down again.

'What's the matter with you, Lola?' he said. 'The world has changed. You're a modern girl. You must look forwards, not backwards. And nature's not all that wonderful, when you think about it. Man is the most intelligent animal there is, and if we can control nature – make it work better – why not?'

Lola stared at him in silence. Was she imagining it, or did his voice sound harder? How well did she really know him? And how many of these 'new world' people were there? Did they all think like Sim? 'When you begin such things, where do you stop?' Her grandmother's words danced before her eyes, and the coldness inside her turned to fear.

Sim stood up and came over to her. He looked down into her face. 'Stop worrying,' he said, smiling. 'I married you for your blue eyes and your quick brain, not for some silly old ideas in your grandmother's notebook.' He put his warm, strong arms around her. 'Come on,' he said gently. 'Let's go down and watch the river sports from an air taxi.'

As they waited on the roof for the air taxi, Lola watched her husband's thin, intelligent face. She loved him. What would she do without him? And of course Sim loved her. She pushed the fear inside her away. It was ridiculous to be afraid. Sim was right. Of course things were different now. Life was always changing – new ideas, new methods. Her grandmother's warning about a dangerous and frightening world was silly. It was all quite natural really. There was nothing to worry about.

Exercises

1 Read through the story quickly and find this information.

1 The year when Sally wrote her letter to her granddaughter, Lola.
2 Lola's age when her grandmother wrote the letter.
3 The year when Sally Gardiner met Milo.
4 The name of the head teacher at Sally's school.
5 The number of countries Milo had lived in.
6 Lola's age when her grandmother died.
7 The name of Sally's husband.
8 Lola's job.
9 The year when Lola read her grandmother's letter.
10 The colour of Michael's hair.

2 Are these sentences true (√) or false (x)?

1 Sally had four older brothers.
2 Sally liked being part of a big family.
3 Sally's brother Michael wanted to be a doctor.
4 Milo could go out of his school whenever he liked.
5 Milo did not work very hard at his school.
6 Milo wanted to know everything about Sally's life and family.
7 Milo's school was a special school for children with learning difficulties.
8 At first Lola did not believe Sally's story about Milo.
9 Sim was one of the 'new world' people.
10 Sim wanted to have children.

3 Comprehension questions

1 What was Lola doing in Sally's garden on 1st January 2050?
2 Why didn't Sally want Lola to read her notebook in 2050?
3 How old was Sally when she wrote the letter?
4 What did Sally's brother Tom like doing?
5 Who was Old Bill Hayes?

6   What did Sally teach?

7   What astonished Sally about Milo the first time they met?

8   Why did Milo like hearing about Sally's family?

9   How did Sally find out about the school at Batworthy?

10 Why did Old Bill think that Jean Nuttall was a bit mad?

11 What did Sally plan to say if she got into the school at Batworthy?

12 What did Sally begin to feel when she was at the school gates?

13 How did Milo get out of the school secretly?

14 Who was Milo's 'mother'?

15 What was the purpose of the experiment in genetic engineering?

16 Why did the scientists keep this experiment so secret?

17 Why didn't the other children at the school try to escape?

18 How was Milo different from other children at the school?

19 Why was Sally terribly afraid for Milo?

20 Why wouldn't Milo go home with Sally?

21 Why did Sally want to talk to her friend Angela?

22 What happened while Sally was seeing Angela in London?

23 Why wouldn't the police look for Milo?

24 What did other people say to Sally about Milo?

25 Why, at the end of her life, did Sally change her mind about Milo's story?

26 Why did Sally want to warn Lola?

27 How long did Lola know Sim before they got married?

28 What did Sim want in life?

29 What had Sally and Michael joked about together in their old age?

30 What did Sim think was the purpose of genetic engineering?

4   Who in the story said, wrote or thought these words?

1   'We will become the leaders of tomorrow's world, the men and women of power.'

2   'They're not going to be very nice people.'

3   'Their purpose in life is to be successful, not to be loved.'

4 'Every country in the world has laws to prevent experiments with people.'
5 'I think it will be a dangerous and frightening world to live in.'
6 'When you begin such things, where do you stop?'
7 'Perhaps ordinary people would rather control their own lives.'
8 'Genetic engineering is the most sensible thing that has happened for years.'
9 'Nature's not all that wonderful, when you think about it. If we can control nature – make it work better, why not?'
10 'It was all quite natural really. There was nothing to worry about.'

5 Discussion questions

1 Why did Milo want to live in a family like Sally's? Compare Milo's life with, e.g. Tom's life.
2 If you had been Sally, would you have believed Milo's story? And if you had believed it, what would you have done?
3 What kind of person was Sim? What kind of world did he want? Do you think that anything he said was 'dangerous or frightening'?
4 Why do you think that Lola persuaded herself that there was nothing to worry about? What would you have thought or done in her position?
5 'Nature's not all that wonderful, when you think about it.' Do you agree? Why?/Why not?
6 It is already possible to make small changes to the genes in a human baby before birth (for example, to prevent certain kinds of diseases), but there are laws to control these experiments carefully. Do you think that all experiments in genetic engineering with people should be stopped? Why?/Why not?

Glossary

beauty: being beautiful; loveliness

busybody: someone who takes too much interest in other people's lives

cheerfully: in a happy, friendly way

cottage: a small house in the country

darling: used to speak to someone you love

Department of Education: the part of the government that controls all schools, teaching, etc

experiment: a test done by scientists in order to study what happens

fade: lose brightness and colour

friendship: being friends; having someone as your friend

fright: a sudden strong fear

gene: a very small part of a body or plant that is passed from parent to child and that controls what the child will look like, how tall it will be, etc

genetic engineering: the methods by which scientists change or make new kinds of living things; they put in or take out certain genes, and this causes changes in the 'child' of a plant

get on with (something): continue doing (something)

Goodness!: people say this when they are surprised

Go on!: an idiom that means 'I don't believe you!'

grin: smile in a friendly, cheerful way

have a word with (someone): speak to (someone)

keep (one's) ear to the ground: know what is happening (because you talk and listen to people)

laboratory: a special room or building where scientists work and do experiments

leader: someone who goes in front; an important person who has power and controls things

maths, mathematics: the study of numbers, sizes, shapes, etc

moor: an area of wild, open, rough land on hills

patient: calm and unhurried; able to wait without getting angry

pool: a small area of still water

rent: pay money to live in a house that you do not own

ridiculous: very, very silly; so silly that you can't believe it
scientific: of or belonging to science and scientists
sleepy: (of a place) very quiet and peaceful; not exciting
stream: a small river
take great care: be very careful
wrist: the part of the body where the arm joins the hand